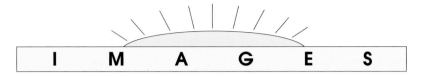

Clothes

Karen Bryant-Mole

Heinemann

First published in Great Britain by Heinemann Library, Halley Court, Jordan Hill, Oxford OX2 8EJ,
a division of Reed Educational & Professional Publishing Ltd.

OXFORD FLORENCE PRAGUE MADRID ATHENS MELBOURNE AUCKLAND KUALA LUMPUR
SINGAPORE TOKYO IBADAN NAIROBI KAMPALA JOHANNESBURG GABORONE
PORTSMOUTH NH (USA) CHICAGO MEXICO CITY SAO PAULO

Designed by Jean Wheeler
Commissioned photography by Zul Mukhida
Produced by Mandarin Offset Ltd.
Printed and bound in China

01 00 99 98 97
10 9 8 7 6 5 4 3 2 1

ISBN 0 431 06306 0

British Library Cataloguing in Publication Data
Bryant-Mole, Karen
Clothes. - (Images)
1.Clothing and dress - Juvenile literature
2.Costume - Juvenile literature   3.Readers (Primary)
I.Title
391

**Some of the more difficult words in this book are
explained in the glossary.**

Acknowledgements
The Publishers would like to thank the following for permission to reproduce photographs. Tony Stone Images; 14 (left)
Jerome Tisne, 15 (right) Andy Sacks, 18 (left and back cover) Jess Stock, (right) Don Spiro, 19 (left) David Madison,
(right) Zigy Kaluzny, 23 (left) Peter Cade, Zefa; 14 (right), 15 (left), 22 (both), 23 (right).

Every effort has been made to contact copyright holders of any material reproduced in this book. Any omissions will be
rectified in subsequent printings if notice is given to the Publisher.

Contents

Materials

Clothes can be made from many different materials.

cotton

4

wool

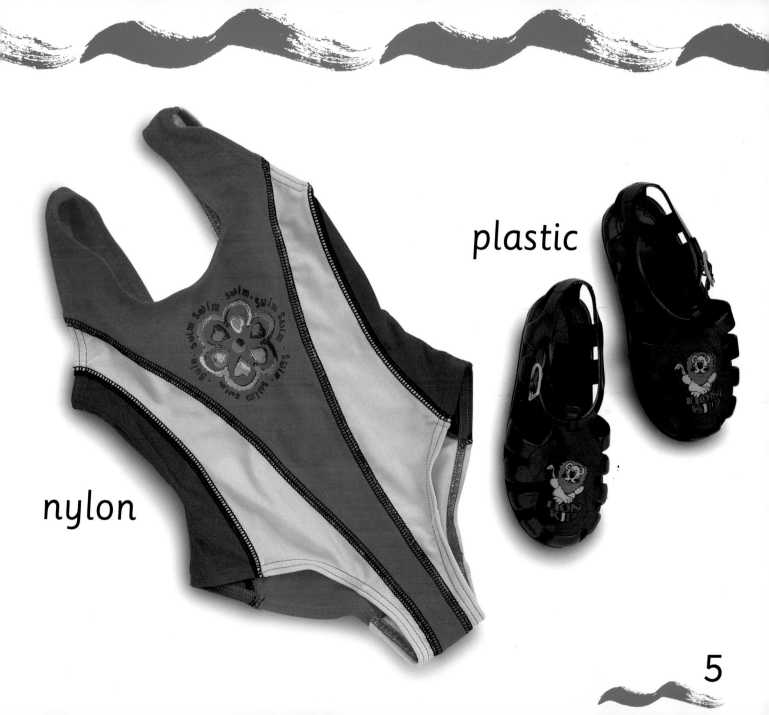

plastic

nylon

5

Fabric

Some of the clothes we wear
are made from **fabric**.

The fabric is cut
into pieces.
The pieces are
then stitched together.

Knitting

These clothes have been knitted.

This jumper has been knitted by machine.

This one
has been
knitted
by hand.

Hot days

Here are some clothes
that will keep you cool
on a hot, sunny day.

11

Cold days

These clothes will keep you warm on a cold day.

13

Nightwear

What do you wear at night?

pyjamas

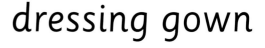

sleeping suits

nightdress

What do you wear at night?

15

Shoes

All of these can
be worn on
your feet.

Sports

You need to wear special clothes to play some sports.

skiing

baseball

karate

soccer

19

Hats

Which of these hats
do you like best?

21

Dressing up

Dressing up in different clothes can be fun.

magician

angel

chef

superhero

Glossary

fabric a type of material, sometimes called cloth
materials what things are made from
stitched sewn together using a needle
and thread

Index